The African Girl God Remembered

MY STORY, YOUR STORY – SILENT BATTLES, COUNTED TEARS, UNBROKEN FAITH

Esther Charity Osemwegie

London Publishing House

Sedona, Arizona

To: _____

From: _____

Healing & Deliverance Blessing

"I pray these pages become a safe refuge for your heart. A reminder that survival is not where your story ends. May the God who lifted this African girl lift you too. May hope return, may courage awaken, and may healing find you in every chapter. You are not forgotten. God remembers you."

The African Girl God Remembered:

My Story, Your Story

Silent Battles, Counted Tears, Unbroken Faith

Copyright © 2026 by Esther Charity Osemwegie.

All rights reserved. No part of this publication may be reproduced, distributed or transmitted in any form or by any means, including photocopying, recording, or other electronic or mechanical methods, without the prior written permission of the publisher, except in the case of brief quotations embodied in critical reviews and certain other noncommercial uses permitted by copyright law. For permission requests, write to the publisher, addressed "Attention: Permissions Coordinator," at the address below.

This book contains reflections drawn from the author's life and includes real-life events and experiences. While the work is grounded in truth, certain names, identifying details, and circumstances have been changed to protect the privacy and identities of individuals involved. Any resemblance to actual persons, living or deceased, beyond these intentional portrayals is coincidental.

Esther Charity Osemwegie
www.theafricangirlgodremembered.com

London Publishing House
PO Box 1223
Sedona, Arizona 86339

ISBN 979-8-9946811-0-7

DEDICATION

This book is dedicated to my mother,
the first woman who carried me
in her body, in her blood, and in her prayers.
Through her, I inherited both the weight of survival
and the quiet strength to endure.
Her life made mine possible.

It is dedicated to my daughter,
the living promise that the story does not end with me.
May you inherit truth without trauma,
love without fear,
and faith without wounds.
May you never have to unlearn your worth
to remember who you are.

And it is dedicated to my husband,
my covering, my witness, and my earthly refuge.
Thank you for loving me in the places
where healing was still in progress,
for standing with me when remembering was painful,
and for choosing me while God restored me.
To the children who came into my life through marriage,
You were a part of God's restoration
A living testimony redeemed through love
and divine covenant.

This work also belongs to the African girl God
remembered
the one who survived, the one who healed,
the one who became a woman
and dared to believe she was never forgotten.

May these pages honor the lineage behind me,
the legacy before me,
and the love that held me together
until God made me whole.

CONTENTS

All to the Glory of God 1
From Survivor to Servant of God 4
    1. Jessie: The Seed of Strength 8
    2. The House of Many Wives 11
    3. Madam Jemimah: My Grandma, The Matriarch 17
    4. The Father I Never Met 22
    5. Big Aunty Margaret: The Enforcer 25
    6. The Curse of Polygamy 28
    7. The Call That Broke the Curse 33
    8. A New Land, A New Beginning 37
    9. When My Innocence was Stolen 40
    10. The Hidden Mother 43
    11. Aunty Jojo: The Servant and the Mother 48
    12. The Shadow Years of Aunty Jojo 51
    13. The Fall of Felix 54
    14. The Long Road to Freedom 60
    15. The Flood that Set Me Free 66
Finding Myself in the Truth 70
    16. A Mother's Pain, A Daughter's Promise 73
    17. God's Surprise: A New Beginning 77
    18. Forgiveness: My Hardest Victory 82
    19. The Battle for My Mind 88
    20. The Year I Finally Chose Myself 93
    21. Breaking Curses and Claiming Destiny 97
    22. God Is Always on Time 103
My Heart's Reflection 105
For the Reader 107

ACKNOWLEDGMENTS

Special thanks to all the dear beloved friends and families that God used in shielding me and all mine during our years in the caves and wilderness journeys. Their homes were a safe haven for me and my offspring thus we thank you all so much!

A very special thanks to my Beta Readers. Your dedication and feedback have been extremely impactful to the success of this project.

May the Almighty Father God reward you all on behalf of me and all mine in Jesus Mighty Name we pray – Amen!

The eternal battle continues and to our Jehovah God who is victorious and has never lost a battle be all the glory both now, forever and ever – Amen.

> "I am the Lord: that is my name: and my glory will I not give to another, neither my praise to graven images."
>
> Isaiah 42:8

*Whoever conceals their sins does not prosper,
but the one who confesses and renounces them
finds mercy.*
Proverbs 28:13

PROLOGUE

All to the Glory of God

TODAY, I STAND in the light of victory. What was designed to break me has become the very testimony that lifts me. I am no longer the terrified girl of an orphan, nor the voiceless teenage immigrant who carried shame that did not belong to her. I am a wife, a mother, a woman established by the hand of God. I am the living proof that the devil can throw every weapon he has and still fail, because God's purpose cannot be stopped. Hallelujah!

This is my true life story. A story of every trap the enemy set to destroy me and how God stepped in, shut the mouth of the wicked, and turned every evil into good for me, for my children, and for the generations after us. There were nights I wanted to end my life. Nights I felt forgotten. Days I questioned why God chose such a painful path for a girl like me. Yet even then, God held me. He never let go. Romans 8:28 says, "All things work together for good to them that love God, to them who are called according to His purpose," and I am walking, breathing evidence that this scripture is true.

I write this book as a testimony and a lifeline. For the young girl who thinks she is alone. For the woman who feels trapped by generational bondage. For the person who wonders if God sees their silent tears. For the believer growing weary in the fight. I want you to know what I had to learn by surviving the impossible: do not run from God when life turns dark. Run toward Him. He is the Rescuer. He is the Redeemer. He is the One who makes the enemy's plot become the doorway to purpose.

Like Joseph, I was betrayed by those I trusted. I was brought into a life meant to enslave me. Yet the same God who raised Joseph from the pit to the palace lifted me from trauma to triumph. My story declares that bondage can be broken. Curses can be reversed. Families can be restored. God can build a throne where the devil tried to bury a child. Genesis 50:20 says:

> "You meant evil against me; but God meant it for good, to save many lives."

My purpose is bigger than my pain. My testimony is bigger than my past. My healing is meant to unlock healing in others. So, if you are reading this, it is not by accident. May every chapter remind you that God is still writing victorious endings. May hope rise in you again. May you believe that your story is not over.

My story may come off to some as me holding back or trying not to offend, however, I want to honor God and encourage those that are attached to this bloodline. Those who would be affected by my story.

To God be all the glory, forever and ever. Hallelujah and Amen!

INTRODUCTION

From Survivor to Servant of God

BEFORE YOU TURN to another page, I want you to understand something clearly. This book is not written out of bitterness or shame. It is written from a healed place, from a victorious place, from a place where God has made me whole again. Every word is a testimony that the enemy failed.

I did not choose the pain I endured. I did not choose betrayal, abuse, or the generational curse that tried to continue through me. I did not choose the lies, the fear, or the darkness that overwhelmed my young life. Yet God chose me. He chose me to live. He chose me to rise. He chose me to be a witness of His power to restore what was violently stolen.

There were moments I wanted to give up. Moments where death looked like relief. Times when I cried out asking God why He allowed these things to happen to me. I was just a child. I was naïve. I was unequipped. Still, God preserved me because He knew the woman I would become. He knew I would tell the truth and bring others to freedom.

This book is written for five purposes:

1. **Healing.** To remind the broken that God cares about the wounds no one sees.
2. **Encouragement.** To strengthen those who are weary in battle.
3. **Awareness.** To protect young girls from wolves pretending to be sheep.
4. **Ministry.** To show that deliverance is real and God restores the stolen years.
5. **Legacy.** To mark the beginning of generational blessings for families that once carried curses.

Forgiveness plays a powerful role in my story. It did not come overnight. It was a process. It meant releasing those who hurt me and refusing to allow bitterness to bury my destiny. It meant trusting God to heal my mind from suicidal and even homicidal thoughts birthed out of torture. Forgiveness saved my life. Forgiveness set me free.

As you read, you will see the parallels to the life of Joseph. He was betrayed by those who should have loved him. Sold into slavery. Forced to endure injustice and humiliation. Yet God was with him in every season, positioning him for destiny. The same God who elevated Joseph is the God who lifted me from the life the enemy planned to a life designed by heaven.

If you are a believer, I pray your faith will multiply. If you do not yet know Jesus, I pray you will meet Him in these pages. No matter who you are or what you have endured, there is victory available for you too. God is not finished with your story.

> For God so loved the world, that he gave his only begotten Son, that whosoever believeth in him should not perish, but have everlasting life.
>
> John 3:16
>
> That if thou shalt confess with thy mouth the Lord Jesus, and shalt believe in thine heart that God hath raised him from the dead, thou shalt be saved.

For with the heart man believeth unto righteousness; and with the mouth confession is made unto salvation.

Romans 10:9-10

Let this testimony be proof that even when life tries to break you, God can use every shattered piece to build something glorious. The pain was real. The process was long. The scars remain, but so does the glory.

So, turn the page and walk with me. See how far God has brought me. See what He has done. See who He is.

Let this truth sink in: Your pain does not disqualify your purpose. It may be the very path to it.

Psalm 118:17 declares:

"I shall not die, but live, and declare the works of the Lord."

All praise to God. Always. Amen and Amen

CHAPTER 1

Jessie: The Seed of Strength

MY STORY BEGINS before my birth. To understand who I am and what God has done in my life, you must first understand the life of my beloved mother. Her journey laid the foundation of faith, resilience, and survival that flows through my veins today.

In a small village in Africa, in the year 1932, a baby girl named Jessie was born to her happily married parents, the Onyekweres. When Jessie was only two years old, both of her parents passed away, leaving her an orphan. The community believed deeply in the saying: "It takes a village to raise a child." That became Jessie's reality as aunts, uncles, and neighbors stepped in to raise the little girl whose life had barely begun.

Due to Jessie's parents' death, she never attended any formal form of schooling nor received an education but, Jessie understood what Africans called "pigeon" or broken English. In America, pigeon would be considered a slang language.

It's hard for me to imagine what it must have been like for my mother, Jessie, only a baby, barely learning to walk to lose both of her parents before she could even form a memory of their faces. In an African village, life was already a daily struggle, but for a child without a mother's arms to hold her or a father's voice to guide her, it must have felt like the world had forgotten her. The cries of hunger, the nights without comfort, the absence of a parent's love, these were the beginnings of her story.

And yet, somehow, in the midst of that loss, God placed her in a community that refused to let her vanish into grief. Though she would never know the warmth of her parents' embrace, the village became her family. Still, I can only imagine the quiet ache she must have carried, watching other children run into their mothers' arms while she stood alone, learning far too early that love sometimes comes through the hands of strangers. That kind of pain, the kind that begins before memory weaves itself deep into the soul. It shapes strength in ways the world cannot see.

As Jessie grew older, her life was marked by endurance and quiet strength. Without parents to guide her, she learned early that survival meant serving others with grace and respect. Though life in the village was often harsh, Jessie's spirit remained gentle. She found purpose in hard work and gratitude in small acts of kindness from those who took her in. By the age of fifteen, that same humility and diligence opened a new path, one that would change her life forever.

CHAPTER 2

The House of Many Wives

JESSIE WAS BROUGHT to the family of late Chief Johnson as a maid to one of his wives, Madam Jemimah. In Africa, it is very common and acceptable for the chiefs to have as many wives as they wished and could afford.

When I think about my mother's life at fifteen, I can't help but feel both sorrow and admiration. To be so young, and yet bear the weight of servanthood, is something I can scarcely imagine. While most girls her age were still learning from their mothers, Jessie was already serving in the household of a powerful man, a chief with many wives, many expectations, and a home filled with matrimonial and family.

Yet even in that environment, my mother's character shone brighter than her circumstances. She worked not out of bitterness, but with a quiet strength only God could give.

Her humility and grace became her protection. What others may have seen as lowly work, God used as preparation. Every dish she washed, every floor she swept, and every respectful word she spoke was molding her spirit for a greater purpose.

Later, due to Jessie's good behavior, character, and faithful service to the entire family, she was married as an additional wife to the Chief Johnson. At that time, Chief Johnson was known to already have more than ten wives.

Madam Jemimah was blessed with two biological daughters of her own, Margaret and Beatrice. Jessie herself was blessed by God with four biological children: three sons and one daughter. Her sons were named Chidi, Beks, and Special. Her only daughter is me, Esther. My brother Chidi preceded my mother to eternity, but his memory remains a part of our family's heartbeat.

From an early age, before I even started school, I remember tagging along with my mother to her workplace at the Jim Nursery Flowers. Later, when she started her restaurant business, my mornings began at 6 a.m., following her 5 a.m. prayers and cooking. After praying, I would chew on a local chewing stick, our version of a toothbrush and toothpaste, then sweep the rooms, kitchen, and entire compound (yard) with a local broom, gathering the dirt with a dustpan and dump it in the family dump site at the back of the house. Next came washing the dishes from the night before, helping my mother cook, carrying the pots of food to her shop, and returning home to wash all the cooking utensils used, pots, pans, spoons etc.

Once the chores were done, I would boil hot water on an open fire to bathe and prepare for school. My mother always left food for me before she left for work. I walked to school daily, and when I arrived late, the senior gatekeepers punished all the late comers by making us kneel down for 10-15 minutes or flogging our hands, backs, or buttocks.

Each day when I would get back from school, I would go to the house to take off my school uniform and change into regular clothing, then go to my mom's restaurant to greet her, to eat lunch and wash all the dishes used by her customers and help tidy up the restaurant. When I was done, she would dictate to me the things that needed to be purchased at the market. After I wrote down the grocery list, she would give me the money to go grocery shopping. When I was younger, my mother used to go to the market with me thereby showing and training me on how to shop plus whom the regular sellers are that she bought the food stuff from, and these sellers knew me too.

After making the grocery list, I would then catch the public transportation to and from the market carrying the purchased groceries on my head in a basket. Upon getting home, the chores for the next day would start including going to fetch the water from the home of people that had and sold running water at their house for cash. I would usually go with several empty gallons in a wheelbarrow to fetch the water, making several trips until at least 2-3 barrels were filled up. This water was used for cooking and served to customers at the restaurant. This was my daily routine six days a week. Our day off was Sunday, and my mother made sure that we went to the church every Sunday and other days.

As far back as I can remember, my mother always suffered from knee pain. While cooking or preparing food, she would tie her headscarf around both knees to ease the pain. I often cried watching her struggle, and sometimes she would take medicine when the pain became unbearable. It was only when I grew older that I learned she had arthritis, a silent battle she carried with grace.

Although Jessie had become one of Chief Johnson's wives, she remained a servant in the household. She continued to serve both Madam Jemimah and Chief Johnson with humility. She would trek miles every morning to fetch water from the riverside, farm acres of land for the family, and even work as a laborer on other people's farms to earn extra wages. Whatever she could buy or sell to sustain us, she did.

Even as an orphan, Jessie understood the power and value of education. She was determined that her four children would have the opportunities she never had, even if it meant sacrificing her own comfort. Yet, despite her marriage to Chief Johnson, his family never truly accepted her. To them, she was still a maid. When Chief Johnson's first daughter, Maragret was married years later to Chief Marcus; it was Margaret's dowry payment that was used to marry Jessie into the family. To them, that diminished Jessie's worth. In their eyes, she was never a wife, only a servant.

But my mother refused to accept that narrative. She would not allow her children to live under the label of servitude. With courage and determination, she started a small restaurant business, cooking and selling traditional African meals: rice and stew, beans, fried fish, meats, plantains, fufu, soups of many kinds, akara, moi-moi, groundnuts, bananas, and bread. Through hard work, she provided for her family and taught us the value of perseverance.

Jessie also understood the importance of faith. She became a devoted member of the Anglican Church, faithfully attending services and ensuring her children were raised in the fear of the Lord. Despite her arthritis and aging body, she continued to clean the church on Saturdays, attend women's meetings, and serve wherever she was needed. Her faith never wavered.

Until the day she went home to be with the Lord Jesus Christ, Jessie lived as a woman of strength, devotion, and unwavering faith. She left behind a legacy of love, hard work, and godliness that continues to live through us, her children and descendants. Her story is one of grace, endurance, and divine favor, a reminder that even the humblest beginnings can produce the most powerful testimonies

CHAPTER 3

Madam Jemimah: My Grandma, The Matriarch

GRANDMA JEMIMAH, Aunty Margaret, Jessie and me, lived under the same roof, but not everyone shaped my childhood in the same way. Within our shared household, Grandma Jemimah became my place of refuge, the source of warmth, safety, and tenderness that softened a world governed by hierarchy and control.

My mother, Jessie, remained part of the household, but like many women in our family structure, her authority over me was shaped by those above her.

To my mother, she was Madam Jemimah, but to me, she was Grandma. Though she was not my grandmother by blood, Grandma Jemimah was the only grandmother I ever knew. My mother, Jessie, had been an orphan who found work as a maid in Madam Jemimah's home, a position that would later lead her into the complex folds of my father's polygamous household. Yet, despite the tangled nature of our family's beginnings, Madam Jemimah never made me feel like an outsider. She embraced me as her own grandchild, and in her presence, I found warmth, structure, and a kind of love that felt pure and unquestioning. My childhood memories are stitched together with her laughter, her gentle discipline, and the sound of her sewing machine humming late into the evening.

Grandma Jemimah was a seamstress by profession, and she expressed her love through every piece of clothing she made. I remember her sewing Easter and Christmas dresses for me each year, carefully crafting them from bright, beautiful fabrics. As she grew older, her eyesight began to fail, and threading with the sewing machine became a challenge. Whenever she called my name to help, I would drop whatever I was doing and run joyfully to her side. I loved being useful to her, loved that she trusted me with even the smallest task.

Africans believe in teaching children responsibility from an early age, and I was no exception. From about the age of five, I slept beside Grandma Jemimah each night. She used to laugh in the mornings, teasing me about how I kicked and rolled all over the bed in my sleep. By the time I turned ten, I began sleeping on a mat in the living room, partly to give her more space and partly to avoid "beating" her with my restless sleep.

Our home had a family outhouse, just a simple hole in the ground, and I made it my duty to bring in a bedpan for Grandma each night, so she wouldn't have to go outside in the dark. Every morning, I emptied it, washed it thoroughly, and left it out to dry, ready for the next night. It was just one of the many ways I cared for her.

Before every meal, I would carefully set her table: a tray with her food, a cup of drinking water, a bowl with soap and water for washing her hands, and a towel to dry them afterward. And no matter how little she had, Grandma always saved some food for me. When I returned from school, the market, or play, she would offer it to me with a proud smile, and I would thank her before happily eating it.

One of her favorite meals was white rice served with Titus sardines and a bottle of Sprite. It felt like a feast every time she shared it with me. Each morning, I would boil water over a wood fire for her bath, gather her sponge and soap basket, and place the stool she sat on while bathing. Afterward, I'd tidy everything back in its place, feeling proud of my little responsibilities.

These routines shaped my sense of care, discipline, and love. To me, they were never chores; they were acts of devotion. Everything I did for Grandma Jemimah was done with joy, because she made me feel safe, loved, and seen in a world that could easily forget a child like me.

My coming to America. In all my years growing up, I had never travelled out of the village to visit any big town or city. But suddenly grace and favor found me and opened a door that is forever a dream for many. I was not even capable of such a dream let alone desiring such or seeing it come to pass. Only God can work such miracles.

The memory of the day I left the village for America remains etched in my heart like a tender scar. Grandma Jemimah held my face in her frail hands; her eyes clouded not just by age but by the weight of parting. "My beloved Ezigbo," she said softly, "wherever you go in life, always learn the good and leave the bad alone." Then she prayed over me, her trembling voice steady with faith and said, "I will miss you, my roommate at night, my errand helper and so much more".

When we embraced, neither of us wanted to let go. We clung to each other, tears streaming down our cheeks, our hearts silently breaking. I can still feel the warmth of her hands on my shoulders, the scent of her skin, and the ache of knowing that our goodbye was more than a separation. It was a farewell between two souls deeply bounded by love.

I remember it like it was yesterday. Leaving Grandma Jemimah was more than leaving a person; it was leaving behind the foundation of who I was. Her love had been my compass, her wisdom my quiet guide. In America, I would come to understand how deeply her presence had shaped me, her tenderness, her discipline, her belief in doing good even when life offered little kindness. The distance between us became a measure of my growing up, but the memory of her prayers followed me everywhere, like an invisible thread stitching my past to my future. Though our worlds were oceans apart, the lessons she planted in me became the roots that kept me steady in every storm.

Life with Grandma Jemimah taught me love, gentleness, and care. Lessons that would later stand in sharp contrast to what awaited me for the rest of my life.

Grandma Jemimah herself was deeply loved by her family, her grandchildren, and all who knew her. When she passed into eternity, she was properly mourned and laid to rest with honor. Her body was taken back to her hometown, the village where she was born, so that she could be buried among her ancestors, just as the tradition required.

CHAPTER 4

The Father I Never Met

AFTER GRANDMA JEMIMAH, the warmth of home took on a different shape. I began to see the weight of hierarchy, tradition, and expectation. Lessons that came not through affection, but through service. That world revolved around my father, Chief Johnson, and his first daughter, Big Aunty Margaret.

Chief Johnson was Madam Jemimah's husband. Together, they had the older of their two daughters, named Margaret. Chief Johnson was also my mother Jessie's husband. According to family history, Chief Johnson died during the Nigerian Civil War. I was born after the war, so I never got to see nor meet him.

What I came to understand later was that Chief Johnson was not just a man within his household; he was a man of authority far beyond it. As a Paramount Chief in Nigeria during the 1950s/60s, he stood at the highest level of traditional leadership in his region. His role placed him above village and clan chiefs, making him the final voice in matters of custom, land, and communal justice. He was the custodian of ancestral laws, responsible for preserving traditions passed down through generations, and ensuring they were upheld even as Nigeria itself was changing after independence from Great Britain.

In those years following independence and during the aftermath of the war, Paramount Chiefs carried an especially heavy burden. Chief Johnson served as a bridge between the old world and the new. Between ancient customs and a modern nation rebuilding itself. He presided over disputes, resolved conflicts among families and villages, and safeguarded communal land that was considered sacred inheritance rather than personal property. His word carried weight not because of force, but because of honor, lineage, and trust.

As a Paramount Chief, he also represented his people beyond his local community. Speaking on their behalf in councils, liaising with government authorities, and protecting his community's interests during a time when political boundaries and power structures were shifting. Chiefs like Chief Johnson were stabilizing figures, grounding their people when uncertainty threatened to erase identity and order.

The Nigerian Civil War was a time of great loss and confusion. So many lives were taken in the chaos, and people were often buried wherever they took their last breath, since traveling with the dead was nearly impossible. After the war ended, the family could not rest knowing that a man of his stature, a respected Paramount Chief, had not been given an honorable burial. According to the African tradition, a Chief must be laid to rest in his own homeland, among his ancestors. So, his body was later exhumed and brought back to his compound (yard), where the family gathered to give him the dignified burial he deserved. It was not only about tradition, but it was also about restoring balance, honor, peace, and respect to his memory.

A Paramount Chief's burial is a sacred act, believed to ensure peace for both the living and the departed. By returning him home, the family honored not just the man he was, but the leadership he embodied, the people he served, and the legacy he left behind.

CHAPTER 5

Big Aunty Margaret: The Enforcer

LIVING UNDER ONE ROOF did not mean living under one experience. While Grandma Jemimah gave me tenderness, Big Aunty Margaret governed my days with discipline, expectations and fear.

Among the many children of Chief Johnson, Madam Jemimah's (eldest) daughter, Margaret, held a place of great authority. In Africa, the younger ones are raised to serve their elders without complaint or hesitation. Margaret was the firstborn daughter of Chief Johnson and the oldest among more than thirty step-siblings, including myself. In our culture, addressing elders by their first names is considered disrespectful, so we all called her Big Aunty Margaret.

Because my mother Jessie had once served as a maid to Madam Jemimah, it was only natural in our family structure that I, too, became a servant to Big Aunty Margaret. Every morning, I rose before dawn to boil water for her tea and breakfast, prepare her bath, and check upstairs to see if she was awake. Once she came down for her bath, she would tell me what she wished to wear for the day. I would search through her many suitcases to find the exact outfit she described, then press it carefully with the charcoal iron, and arrange her lotions, creams, and jewelry for when she returned upstairs to dress.

After school, I went straight to her room never to play, never to rest, but to make her bed, sweep the floor, and ensure everything was in perfect order. In the evenings, I prepared her dinner and cleaned up afterward. Like Grandma Jemimah, Aunty Margaret also used a bedpan at night, which I made sure was always ready for her before bedtime. In the morning, I would take it outside to dump, wash, and dry it before returning it to her room.

These duties were not optional. In our home, chores were to be completed without reminders. Forgetfulness or delay was seen as being incompent, irresponsible, or even rebellious, all of which carried consequences.

Big Aunty Margaret's authority was absolute. None of us dared to question her. She was the kind of woman who could command silence with a single glance. If any of the younger siblings gave their mothers trouble, it took only one report to Aunty Margaret to set things straight. Most of us would rather receive a spanking than be reported to her, because her name alone carried more power than any punishment could.

To me, Aunty Margaret represented the other side of family life, not the tenderness of Grandma Jemimah's care, but the discipline and hierarchy that shaped much of my upbringing. Through her, I learned how obedience was woven into love, how silence could be a form of survival, and how strength could hide behind quiet submission.

Serving Big Aunty Margaret taught me the other side of love, the kind that is bound by duty, silence, and expectations. In her world, affection was measured by obedience, and respect was shown through hard work. Though the weight of those days often pressed on my young shoulders, they shaped my endurance and sharpened my awareness of power, hierarchy, and human nature. Looking back, I realize that every early lesson from threading Grandma Jemimah's sewing needle to attending to Aunty Margaret's endless demands was quietly preparing me for a life where strength would not come from comfort, but from perseverance.

CHAPTER 6

The Curse of Polygamy

AFTER YEARS OF SERVING under Big Aunty Margaret's roof, I came to understand the complexities of our lineage, a family rooted in tradition, power, and pain. While Grandma Jemimah had shown me love, and Aunty Margaret had taught me discipline, life would soon show me how fragile both could be in the face of betrayal and human weakness.

About the age of sixteen or eighteen, Margaret was betrothed to another Chief named Chief Marcus. The arrangement was not born of love or choice, but of tradition. A decision made by her father, Chief Johnson. Chief Marcus was a man old enough to be her father, and like many men of his status, he was already a polygamist with several wives.

The traditional marriage ceremony was grand and filled with community cultural celebrations and rituals, including prayers by elders to bless the union. After the rites were completed, Margaret (now Mrs. Margaret Marcus) was escorted to her husband's home, where his other wives received and welcomed her as the newest addition to their household.

The betrayal. Within two years, the young bride gave birth to a baby boy named Felix Marcus. In our culture, visiting family requires no invitation or notice. So, when Margaret had her baby, Beatrice (Margaret's younger sister) came to visit, not just to celebrate the birth, but to help care for the newborn and support her sister through the tender early days of motherhood according to tradition and culture.

But tragedy struck in the most heartbreaking form of betrayal. Chief Marcus, her husband, took an interest in Beatrice and soon after, Beatrice became pregnant by him. To avoid bringing shame upon the family, Chief Marcus was pressured to marry Beatrice as well. Thus, the two sisters became wives to the same man; a mirror of the biblical story of Leah and Rachel (Genesis 29:1–35).

Like Leah and Rachel, envy and heartbreak defined their relationship until their final days. Though sisters by blood, the deep wound caused by the betrayal and forced marriage poisoned their bond. Scripture was fulfilled in their lives:

> "For where jealousy and selfish ambition exist, there will be disorder and every evil practice." James 3:16

Margaret was devastated by what had happened between her and Beatrice. The humiliation and pain were too much for her young heart to bear. She fled from her marriage, from the home that had become her prison, determined to reclaim some sense of dignity.

Later, she remarried another man named John, and God blessed her with another son, Uzoma. But this new marriage soon became another battlefield. John, consumed by jealousy and suspicion, accused Margaret of infidelity. One night, in a fit of rage, he tried to butcher her in her sleep with a knife. But, God intervened.

> "There shall no evil befall thee, neither shall any plague come near thy dwelling." Psalm 91:10

Margaret miraculously survived the attack and spent many months in the hospital recovering. When she was finally discharged, her family especially her father, Chief Johnson welcomed her back home with open arms. They gave her a small one bedroom upstairs in the brick house so she could live safely amongst her kinsmen and recover from the horror she had endured.

In African tradition, however, children belong to the father's lineage. When a marriage ends whether through divorce, death, or separation, the mother is often expected to leave her children behind with their father's family. Rarely does a woman have the right to take her children with her, and she considers herself fortunate if she is ever allowed to see them again.

In both of Margaret's failed marriages, she was forced to leave her sons behind. Each boy was raised by his father's family households steeped in the same generational curses that had plagued our lineage for decades.

In a polygamous family, most of the time, there are all sorts of countless sins, wickedness and atrocities such as envy, jealousy, witchcraft, voodoo, cheating, extramarital affairs with and among the men and maid servants, adultery, fornication, poisoning, false accusations, molestations, incest among step siblings etc. These sins happen so often that it almost becomes normal except for the few of the polygamous family members that might have the true fear of God and refuse to participate in all the ungodly sins and lifestyles.

"For where envying and strife is, there is confusion and every evil work".

James 3:16

The story of Margaret and Beatrice became a living parable in our family, a warning of what happens when power and desire override love and integrity. As a child, I could not yet name it, but I could feel the spiritual heaviness that polygamy carried a pattern of broken hearts, wounded women, and fatherless children repeating across generations. Watching their lives unfold taught me to recognize the quiet dangers hidden in tradition, and to understand that not all customs are sacred. Some are simply chains disguised as heritage.

CHAPTER 7

The Call That Broke the Curse

IN THE HEART OF AFRICA, the rhythm of life moved to the pulse of tradition. Drums, laughter, and prayers filled the air, but so did whisper of pain; the kind passed down through generations like an unspoken inheritance. In a family shaped by polygamy and shadowed by jealousy, envy, and betrayal, one young man dared to rise above it all. His name was Felix Marcus, the first son of Mrs. Margaret Marcus.

Felix was born into a lineage tangled with ancestral battles, spiritual and emotional alike. Yet from an early age, it was clear that God's hand was upon him. While others around him were caught in the cycles of family conflict and the sins that came with polygamy, Felix's heart was drawn toward the things of God. He found joy in prayer, worship, and service. Where confusion ruled, he brought peace. Where resentment lingered, he offered forgiveness. It was as if heaven had marked him for a different path.

> ...visiting the iniquity of the fathers upon the children and upon the children's children unto the third and to the fourth generation."
>
> Exodus 34:7

But Felix was proof that the chain could be broken.

As a young man, Felix became a vibrant minister in the United Church of Christ (UCC) in one of the towns in Africa. His preaching drew crowds not because of eloquence, but because of an anointing that cut through people's hearts. He preached about redemption, healing, and freedom.

By divine favor, Felix was among the few chosen to attend Morris Cerullo's Bible School in San Diego, California an honor that forever changed the course of his life. It was as if God Himself was calling him out of the soil of ancestral bondage into a new inheritance of grace and purpose.

In America, Felix immersed himself in the study of Scripture and ministry. Students from Bible schools across the country often gathered for fellowship, worship, and revival services. During one of those gatherings at Tyler, Texas on the campus of faith Bible school, Felix met a young woman named Denise. Their meeting was not by chance it was destiny.

Their friendship blossomed into love, and after completing their studies, they decided to marry despite the objections of Denise's parents. Their wedding took place, a simple but joyous ceremony that united two hearts and two nations under one God.

Shortly after they were married, Felix returned to Africa with his American wife. Their arrival was a celebration with drums beating, women dancing, relatives gathering in joy. They were welcomed not only as family but as living proof that God's favor could reach across oceans. I was among those who served and cared for Denise, attending to her every need during their stay. She carried herself with grace and humility, and I admired the peace she seemed to bring into our often-turbulent family compound (yard). But they promptly returned to America after the brief visit.

Then, sometime in 1985, Felix decided it was time for his mother, Margaret, to visit him and his wife in the United States. It was an act of love a son honoring the woman who had suffered so much yet never lost her faith. Preparations were made, prayers were said, and to my great surprise and by divine arrangement I, Esther, the only daughter of the orphan Jessie, was chosen to accompany my Big Aunty Margaret on this journey to America.

At that time, I was just an innocent teenager, curious, and completely unaware that this single trip would alter the entire course of my destiny. I did not know that stepping onto that plane meant stepping into the fulfillment of a divine plan that had begun long before I was born.

Felix's journey was more than a story of opportunity; it was the fulfillment of prophecy. God had reached into a bloodline tangled by sin and sorrow and raised up a voice of deliverance. Through him, the curse of polygamy met the cross of redemption. His calling proved that no matter how deep the wounds of the past were, grace could still reach deeper. And in God's perfect plan, that same grace would soon pull me a young girl from the dust of Africa into the light of a new beginning.

CHAPTER 8

A New Land, A New Beginning

IT WAS JANUARY OF 1986, a cold, snow covered morning when our plane descended through thick white clouds into Saint Louis, Missouri. The sight of snow amazed me. I had never seen anything like it, white blankets covering the earth as far as my eyes could see. I pressed my face to the window, watching the frozen landscape below, filled with awe and quiet anticipation. This was America, the land I had only heard about in stories, the place of opportunity, freedom, and new beginnings.

Beside me sat my Big Aunty Margaret, serene and thoughtful. The long journey had exhausted her, but her eyes held peace. For both of us, this was more than a trip; it was crossing a journey from pain into promise. I didn't know then that God was setting the stage for events that would shape the rest of my life.

At the St. Louis Airport, we were greeted by Felix, my Aunt Margeret's son, and his American wife Denise. Felix was confident and polite, a man who seemed used to leadership. Denise's warmth immediately made me feel safe; her smile softened the strangeness of this new land. Felix owned and operated an international business that required frequent travel. He relied heavily on his secretary, Sheila, who had also come to the airport that day. Sheila was friendly and organized, the kind of woman who always seemed to know what to do. In time, I would earn a little spending money by helping her with small household tasks doing laundry and ironing her clothes.

America was beautiful but overwhelming. The language, the food, even the quiet hum of the refrigerator at night felt foreign. I often sat by the window, watching snow fall under the streetlights, wondering what my life would become in this strange land.

Within six months to a year, Aunty Margaret returned to Africa, leaving me in Felix and Denise's care. They wanted me to have time to adjust and learn English before starting school, so I stayed home for nearly a year. Later, they enrolled me at Gateway Christian School in St. Louis, Missouri, beginning in the tenth grade.

Each morning, Denise dropped me off on her way to work. After school, I walked to the school daycare center nearby, where I worked for a few hours before they picked me up. Our routine felt stable, and in those early days, I believed I was exactly where God wanted me to be. At that time, I was their only "child," and they treated me as family.

For the first time, I felt hopeful. Life in America seemed like a fresh start, a chance to dream, to belong, and to grow.

Then came my 16th birthday, a day that remains unforgettable. Felix and Denise's business friends, Don and Karen, hosted a surprise celebration at their home. Karen had baked a beautiful homemade cake, and as everyone sang "Happy Birthday," I was overwhelmed with gratitude. It was the first time in my life that anyone had ever celebrated me. Their kindness touched a part of my heart that had long been neglected.

I later began babysitting Don and Karen's three children, a job that filled me with joy and gave me a sense of independence. Life felt bright and promising. For a while, I truly believed that my story had turned a corner. But that illusion shattered soon after my birthday.

CHAPTER 9

When My Innocence was Stolen

WHEN WE ARRIVED HOME from the celebration, I went to take a shower before bed. As I stepped out of the bathroom, wrapped in my traditional African cloth, the fabric loosened unexpectedly and accidentally slipped from my body. It happened in a moment, innocent, unintentional, but Felix happened to be in the kitchen and saw me. From that day forward, everything changed.

Felix began manipulating me constantly. He would remind me over and over that he and his American wife, Denise, had been married for many years without children. He emphasized that there had never even been a miscarriage because she had never become pregnant at all. He used their childlessness as a weapon, pressuring me emotionally and trying to justify what he wanted from me, as though I was responsible for fulfilling what he believed was missing in his life. The harassment would not stop.

It continued every single day, for more than a year, as if my body existed for Felix to violate and to satisfy his twisted need to prove himself. I was treated like an object, not a child who deserved protection. Every day felt like another attack on my safety, my dignity, and my innocence.

Finally, one ugly day, I was no longer able to fight him off. Felix forced himself inside of my body and defiled my innocence. From that day forward, it was as though Felix was possessed by a demon. He would defile me at anytime and anywhere. Whenever Denise was not around, which was quite often due to her job. By this time, he had dissolved his business, and Denise was the main bread winner.

When Felix was teaching me how to drive a car for me to get my learner's permit and a driving license, he would defile me even at the corn fields in Illinois. The unexplainable mystery about Felix's behavior was that after each of the sinful acts, he would kneel down weeping bitterly asking me to please forgive him promising never to do it again and yet it kept happening.

It was inconceivable that Felix was a Pastor. And now, the man I had regarded as a guardian and spiritual leader no longer looked at me the same way. The warmth and safety I once felt in that home were replaced by an atmosphere of unease and fear. I couldn't understand it fully then, but I sensed that something sacred had been violated not only my innocence but also the trust that held our small household together.

> "The Lord is close to the brokenhearted and saves those who are crushed in spirit." Psalm 34:18

Looking back now, I see that this was the moment the battle for my soul began the collision between light and darkness that would define my journey for years to come. What was meant to be a season of growth and new beginnings became the crucible through which God would ultimately refine me.

Felix used to wake up very late at night, and he would spend hours writing nonstop. He said God was giving him messages to publish for the Body of Christ. Yet, despite all his claims of spirituality, the ancestral curse of polygamy from both sides of his family seemed to have a powerful hold on him. His behavior showed no evidence of freedom or holiness.

CHAPTER 10

The Hidden Mother

THE MONTHS AFTER my sixteenth birthday became the darkest season of my life. The man I once trusted as a guardian began using his authority to control and manipulate me. Felix, who was both my relative and pastor, reminded me constantly that he and his wife Denise had been married for many years without a child. He repeated their story so often that it began to feel like a warning. He used their pain to justify his actions, to twist my sense of responsibility, and to convince me that I owed him something I could never give.

What began as emotional manipulation soon turned into daily torment. I was no longer treated as a child who deserved protection but as someone whose voice had no power. The fear in that house became my constant companion. Every sunrise felt heavier than the last. The same man who prayed, preached, and claimed to hear from God showed no evidence of freedom or holiness. His heart was still chained by the same ancestral curse of polygamy and marital betrayal that had ravaged our family for generations.

> "The sins of the fathers are visited upon the children to the third and fourth generation." Exodus 34:7

After a year of confusion and silence and sexual molestation/abuse, I discovered I was pregnant. I was only seventeen. The moment I realized the truth, my world collapsed. I had always dreamed of becoming a lawyer and lifting my mother Jessie and my siblings out of poverty. Now those dreams felt stolen. I was terrified and ashamed, too afraid to tell anyone the truth.

When I finally told Felix, he reacted not with remorse but with excitement. He insisted that we create a false story to hide the truth from Denise. I was so frightened that I agreed. Together we fabricated a tale that someone else had violated me. Later, while walking with Denise one afternoon, I broke down in tears and told her that I was pregnant. I couldn't bear the weight of the lie. Denise comforted me and promised that everything would be all right. I didn't know how deeply that falsehood would bind all of our lives together.

As the months passed, Felix began isolating me from others. I was no longer allowed to visit family or friends in other cities. He even gave me strange mixtures to drink that tasted like salt and water, claiming they would help my body. Out of fear, I obeyed, not knowing the damage they might cause. I wasn't sure if those drinks were attempts for a homemade abortion. My health suffered. Later in life, I ended up developing high blood pressure. I believe it was from drinking too many of those concoctions with salt water throughout the pregnancy. Only God knows.

The one thing I held on to and prayed for often was that the child in my womb would be a girl. One who would grow up to break the curse that had haunted our bloodline. I prayed that her life would mark the beginning of something new.

In the month of February 1990, after a Sunday dinner, I started experiencing some stomach pains. I had no idea what they were. The next day, Monday, Felix took me to different donation centers to see if we could find some baby stuff. The stomach pain continued all that day.

By Tuesday, the stomach pain was happening increasingly frequent. After our family dinner, Denise called a family friend, Sheila, who was a nurse, to ask her what she thought of the pain that I was experiencing. Sheila told Denise that they should take me straight to the hospital because it sounded like I was having birth labor pains.

I was driven to Saint Elizabeth Hospital emergency room around seven o'clock in the evening. The doctor confirmed that I was in labor. Within a few hours, I was wheeled into the labor room. When I was fully dilated, the doctor broke my water, and my beautiful, precious, innocent baby girl was born.

Felix was so happy and excited over the birth of his daughter, especially since he and his wife had been unable to have any child of their own. Felix named his precious beloved daughter Ngozi (meaning blessing). My baby girl and I were released from the hospital on Thursday and upon getting home, I had nothing whatsoever for the baby. I sat down on the rocking chair in the living room looking at my baby girl and started crying. I had no idea what to do with my baby girl, Ngozi. Denise had to call Sheila again to help us figure it out because Denise herself did not know how to help me.

Sheila came over that weekend bringing with her a big baby green plastic bathtub to show me how to properly bathe the baby, breastfeed the baby, etc. In the meantime, Felix was running around all over Illinois thrift stores and donation centers collecting all the baby collectibles he could find for his daughter, Ngozi whom his wife Denise had no idea was her husband's biological baby girl.

Ngozi was loved unconditionally beyond measure. Ngozi grew up calling Felix daddy and calling, his American wife, Denise mommy. **She called me Aunty Jojo.**

The situation reminded me of the story of Moses and his mother Jochebed in Exodus 2, a woman who raised her own son while the world never knew the truth. I, too, was a hidden mother.

CHAPTER 11

Aunty Jojo: The Servant and the Mother

THE WORLD AROUND ME CAME TO KNOW ME AS AUNTY JOJO.

To the outside world, I was the cheerful helper. The one who cooked, cleaned, cared for the children, and made sure everyone was all right. They saw only my hands, not my heart. They saw my smile, but not the sorrow behind it. Beneath that name lived a woman carrying a truth too heavy to tell. A mother in disguise.

Avoiding the truth of what actually happened, Felix sent messages to his family and friends and told them that he and his wife had adopted a baby girl named Ngozi.

By the time Ngozi was about two and half years old, Felix and Denise finally had their very own biological son after ten long years of waiting on God. Around the same time, I found myself pregnant again. Just like the first time, Felix did not want anyone to know the sins and the atrocities that he was committing against me. He demanded silence. He feared exposure more than he feared God and he forced me to have an abortion. The abortion was performed under an alias in Saint Louis, Missouri.

I remember the smell of antiseptic in the air and the coldness of that sterile room. My tears fell silently as I prayed for forgiveness and strength. My painful secret life continued, and for the sake of my innocent daughter, Ngozi, I endured each day with quiet sorrow.

Years passed, and Felix and Denise went on to have five children in total. They had two sons and three daughters. Together with Ngozi, all six children were raised as siblings, and I cared for them all as their "Aunty Jojo." To outsiders, we looked like one happy family, picture perfect in church, at school events, and neighborhood and family gatherings. But behind closed doors, only Heaven and I knew the truth buried beneath the surface.

As the family grew, Felix brought his mother, Margaret, back from Africa to help care for the children while Denise continued working to support the household. By then, we had relocated to Oklahoma City.

Because of my unplanned pregnancy, I had been unable to complete high school, but later I found the courage to pursue my GED at Lewis and Clark Community College. It was a small step, yet to me, it represented survival. Each class represented defiance against the darkness that once tried to silence me.

With every page I studied, I felt God whispering, You are still mine. It was as if He was rebuilding me one subject, one chapter, one tear drop at a time. That diploma became more than paper. It was proof that even broken wings could still fly. A glimmer of hope that education and faith could one day help me rise from the ashes of my past.

Through it all, I clung to God's promises. Though I was silenced, God was not. Though I lived as a hidden mother, Heaven knew my name.

"The Lord will fight for you; you need only to be still."

Exodus 14:14

CHAPTER 12

The Shadow Years of Aunty Jojo

THEY CALLED ME "Aunty JoJo." In that name was both love and deception. A mask that allowed me to exist inside the family without explanation. To the world, I was the loyal aunt who cooked, cleaned, braided hair, wiped tears, and held babies through fevered nights. But behind the soft smile of "Aunty JoJo" was a woman trapped in two realities: a mother in secret, and a servant in plain sight.

Felix's house was always full of noise and children's laughter. Amid all of it, I moved silently, folding clothes that were not mine, cooking meals, tucking in little ones who did not know the story behind my tired eyes. My daughter, Ngozi, called me "Aunty" too, and each time the word left her mouth, my heart cracked a little more. To love your child from behind the curtain of shame, was the price of secrecy.

There were times when Ngozi laughed, I saw the part of me that was still alive, still capable of joy despite the silence that had been forced upon me.

In the daylight, I was the housekeeper. At night, I was the invisible wife. I learned how to make my spirit small, how to walk through rooms like smoke. Present, but untouchable. I prayed quietly while scrubbing floors, whispering Bible verses under my breath like medicine: *"The Lord is my shepherd; I shall not want."* The words became a heartbeat, a rhythm that carried me through the long days of servitude.

Faith, like a flickering ember, began to glow again in those hidden prayers. I did not yet believe that freedom was possible, but I believed that God still saw me. That belief , even in whispers, became my rebellion. When Felix's eyes turned cruel or Margaret's commands bit deep, I spoke to God inside my mind, saying, "One day, Lord, You will lift me up. One day, You will make this right."

Strength, for me, was learning to survive without hope. It was forgiving people who never asked for forgiveness.

Sometimes, late at night, I'd watch the moonlight fall across the sleeping children and imagine another life. A small home, laughter without fear, love without conditions. I would picture myself walking freely through a market somewhere, carrying my own basket, answering to no one. Those dreams were the only place I could breathe.

But the world around me was changing. The children were growing, the burdens heavier, and Felix's hold on me began to shift. I sensed that something was coming. A divine interruption that would shatter the years of secrecy and pain.

I didn't know it then, but the night that would change everything was already on its way.

For years, I lived between two worlds. The visible one that served others and the invisible one that prayed for freedom. I did not know that God had been listening all along, collecting every tear and turning them into seeds of deliverance. Even in the silence, even in the shame, my faith was not dead. It was only buried.

CHAPTER 13

The Fall of Felix

WHEN DENISE'S COMPANY transferred her to Oklahoma City, the entire family followed. She was the main breadwinner, the steady one, and we all depended on her to keep the household afloat. The move didn't change much for me, I was still "Aunty JoJo," the caretaker, the invisible servant holding together a family that was never truly mine.

But God sees what man ignores, and the heaven records what the world forgets.

One night in 1998, my years of torment reached the end in a way no one could have imagined. I was sleeping on an air mattress in the children's room when Felix came in again, as he often did so many times before. But in that moment, something shifted. As he reached for me, his body suddenly stiffened and he collapsed. A deep groan escaped his lips, and he fell lifelessly beside me. Felix had a stroke.

Out of sheer panic, I dragged his heavy body into the living room and screamed for Denise and his mother, Margaret. When they rushed in, we found one side of his body completely paralyzed. His speech was slurred, his eyes wild with confusion and rage. Denise and Margaret wanted to call an ambulance, but Felix, still trying to control everything even as his body betrayed him, refused. He ordered them not to call for help, and they obeyed.

From that night forward, Felix never walked again. His once proud voice became broken whispers. The man who once demanded my silence now needed help to speak with every breath. I became his nurse. The same hands that once resisted him now fed him, bathed him, and changed his adult diapers. Pride had brought him low, and God Himself had written the judgment I was too afraid to speak.

Even little Ngozi, only eight years old, helped care for him. She would steady his wheelchair or hand him water, innocent to the truth of who he really was. To her, he was simply "Daddy." To me, he was the living proof that God's justice may come slowly, but it never fails to.

After months of suffering, Felix passed away. By then, we had relocated again. This time to Maryland. He was buried in Pennsylvania near his in-laws. I stood by the grave not as a widow, not even as a recognized mother, but as a quiet witness to the end of a decade of bondage. I did not rejoice; I simply whispered, "You have seen me, Lord."

After his death, I thought the truth would finally set me free. Instead, it was locked away once more. Before Felix died, he had confessed to his mother, my Big Aunty Margaret, that Ngozi was his biological daughter. Margaret, rather than seek forgiveness or make peace, she took me to a hotel room. Denise had reserved it for her not knowing why she wanted to go. She pleaded with me to keep her son, Felix's sin a secret. She never wanted it to be revealed or made public.

Out of fear and the safety of my daughter, Ngozi, I agreed. Silence, once again, became my armor and my prison.

Margaret's cruelty only deepened after Felix's death. She took her anger out on Ngozi, her own granddaughter. She was made to do endless chores: cooking, cleaning, ironing, washing, running errands long into the night while her siblings slept. None of the other children were treated that way.

One night, Margaret struck Ngozi with the heel of her shoe for a small mistake, splitting her head open. Blood ran down her tiny face, and I felt a deep cry rise inside me. Not just for my child, but for every generation of women silenced by fear and power.

The pattern was repeating. I had been her servant as a child in Africa, and now my daughter was carrying the same yoke in America. The same spirit of control and hatred moved through generations like an invisible chain.

Margaret from birth nicknamed me "Akpa-Ego," which means Bag of Money. It was a cruel reminder that her first husband's dowry had been used to marry my mother, Jessie, into her father's family. To her, that meant my mother and I, and now, even my daughter belonged to her forever as indentured servants.

Even after Felix's death, she continued the same hatefulness to me by making sure that all the income that I earned in America was being used to maintain her very expensive life style such as, buying her all sorts of clothing's (both African fabric, wrappers), head ties and Western attire), jewelry, matching shoes and handbags; food such as stock fishes, dry fishes, special groceries, tailoring, dental, bleaching creams, birthday parties etc.

Even when I did not have a job, she made me sponsor her birthday parties using my credit cards. I knew that she was doing this out of hatred so that I did not have any money to send to my mother, Jessie, and my biological siblings in Africa.

Before Felix's death, he had procured over twenty separate credit cards in my name or had me cosigned them. I was buried in debt. But God began to move. I entered a debt relief program and, by His grace, paid off every dollar over five long years without missing a single payment. It was one of the hardest journeys of my life, but it became the beginning of my financial and spiritual redemption and freedom.

Life was very hard feeding from hand to mouth. The African church family DGM that Denise and her family found in Maryland became a family indeed, checking on us and assisting us by whatever means they could.

In those small acts of kindness, my faith began to stir again. For years, I had believed God was silent and that He had turned His face away from me. But in those moments, I felt His presence again, soft but undeniable, reminding me that He had never left.

Looking back, I realize that the night Felix fell was not just the night he lost his life; it was the night God gave me back mine. His death did not erase the years of pain, but it ended his cycle of domination.

I began to understand that deliverance doesn't always come in the form of escape. Sometimes deliverance comes as revelation. What the enemy meant for evil, God was already rewriting for good. (Romans 8:28).

As the prophet, Jeremiah wrote, "Who is he that saith, and it cometh to pass, when the Lord commandeth it not?"

Lamentations 3:37.

For the first time, I believed those words not just in theory, but in truth. No one, not Felix, not Margaret, not fear itself had the final say over my destiny. Only God did.

And He had just begun to speak.

CHAPTER 14

The Long Road to Freedom

FELIX'S DEATH left me standing at the edge of a new life but stepping into it was not easy. When Felix died, Margaret did not return to Africa. She stayed and continued to plant herself inside the home. Felix might be gone, but she still believed she owned everything he touched, including me.

I was still living in the same house with Margaret and Denise, surrounded by the shadows of the life I never chose. I worked constantly, but Margaret controlled the household, the children, everything. Even without Felix's iron grip, the weight of cultural obligation, fear, and years of conditioning kept me trapped. I did not yet know how to stand on my own. I only knew how to survive, while serving.

But something inside me had shifted.

The night Felix fell was the end of his life, but it was the beginning of mine. God had begun stirring my spirit again, awakening in me a belief I thought I had lost forever: the belief that my destiny did not belong to anyone but Him.

And with that belief, I took my first brave step.

I knew that if I wanted a different life for myself and my daughter, Ngozi, I had to find a door that no one, not Felix, not Margaret, not fear could shut. That door was education.

One day, with trembling hands and a determined heart, I walked into Prince George's Community College to ask how I could start school. I was terrified, terrified of failure, of embarrassment, of being too old, too tired, too burdened. But I registered anyway, one class at a time.

I paid for every class myself, working two to three jobs, often coming home so exhausted that I cried into my pillow before forcing myself up again. The two-year Associate degree took me ten years to complete. Ten years of night shifts, early mornings, and walking into class with blistered feet and a prayer on my lips. But I finished.

The Bachelor's degree took another six years. Pay as you go, every penny earned with sweat, with the help of student loans, and with a determination that could only have come from God.

Twelve years passed before I could afford even a single visit back to Africa. Twelve years of missing my mother, missing my siblings, feeling the ache of distance and longing, but pushing forward anyway.

During this time, men began to show interest in marrying me. Some were kind, some serious, some promising. But every time a man came to ask for my hand, Margaret stepped in. She would line up all six of her grandchildren in front of the suitor and, as if I came with a small army, would declare that any man who wanted me must also take full responsibility for all of them and for her as well. No man in his right mind would accept such a burden, and she knew it. It was her strategy: keep me unmarried, keep me available, keep me under her control. I had more than ten suitors. Every single one was chased away.

One man, Onyebuchi seemed different. He seemed serious, and for the first time, I allowed myself to hope. When I became pregnant, he convinced me, under pressure, under fear, under the influence of his family, that the baby must be aborted since we weren't yet married. The abortion was done under an alias, my heart breaking quietly in a cold medical room.

Less than a year later, Onyebuchi traveled to Africa, married a woman chosen by his family, and brought her to America. I carried that pain alone. The grief of another child lost. The humiliation of being deemed "not good enough." The ache of betrayal.

After him came another man, a placeholder from ages thirty to forty, always promising marriage, never delivering anything tangible. He never took me to his home, never introduced me to his family, always claimed to be "traveling." In one year, we saw each other only two or three times at restaurants or at my friend's house. Eventually, I realized I had been holding onto shadows.

I let it go. I let all of it go. Marriage, finally, was no longer my priority. My heart was tired. My spirit was bruised. I chose myself, my education, and my daughter.

Even after Felix's death, Margaret's patterns of control continued, not just with me, but with my daughter, Ngozi. When Ngozi turned sixteen, she began working. And just as Felix had forced me to sign over every paycheck, Margaret demanded the same from Ngozi. My own daughter, a child, was being made to hand over her earnings while Margaret's other five grandchildren kept every penny they made. It broke my heart. It awakened every maternal instinct in me. I knew I had to protect her.

When Ngozi finished middle school and prepared to enter high school, I was terrified. I feared the public school system, its overcrowded classrooms, gangs, bad influences, the danger to a young girl with no father and a controlling grandmother who mistreated her.

I prayed fervently. In my fear and love, I turned to Denise, the woman who had raised Ngozi physically while I remained hidden as "Aunty Jojo."

I begged Denise to help me get Ngozi into a Christian high school. Denise agreed without hesitation. God bless her loving, caring heart.

During the mother-daughter interview at Lanham Christian School, the principal asked Denise a question about Ngozi that Denise could not answer, because the truth would have revealed everything. Ngozi watched this exchange closely. For the first time in her life, she sensed something was off.

That day when I came home from work, Ngozi approached me with eyes full of fear, curiosity, and longing. "Aunty Jojo," she said softly, "tell me everything about my life that I don't know."

My heart nearly stopped.

I wanted to gather her in my arms and pour out the truth. But she was only fifteen. Her world was still forming.

So I told her gently, "Focus on your education. When you graduate from college with your Bachelor's degree, I will tell you everything you want to know about your life."

She accepted my answer with relief, trusting me fully, and went on with her life.

But inside, I carried the weight of that promise like a stone on my chest.

Because one day, I knew, the truth would have to come out.

But even as I poured myself into school, work, and raising my daughter, one thing remained unchanged: I was still living under the same roof with Denise, her children, and my big aunty Margaret. Their presence was a constant reminder of the life I was fighting to escape. I longed for independence, a home of my own, a place where my spirit could breathe.

Yet fear held me tightly, fear of stepping into the unknown, fear of living alone in a country where I had known nothing but control and servitude.

I didn't know it then, but God was already preparing a way. And when that way opened, it came in the most unexpected form: a flood that would wash me out of bondage and carry me into freedom.

CHAPTER 15

The Flood that Set Me Free

I LONGED TO MOVE OUT of Denise's home, away from the noise, the tension, the memories, and especially the oppression of my big aunty Margaret. But wanting freedom and believing I could live alone were two very different things. From the day I arrived in America, I had only known what it was like to live with Felix, Denise and sometimes Margaret. I had never paid rent on my own, never made a decision without the shadow of someone else's control.

So, I stayed, afraid to step into a world I didn't yet feel equipped to navigate.

But God has a way of moving us when we cannot move ourselves.

In 2011, after a simple, ordinary rainstorm, the basement of our home, the place where my room was, began to flood. Water seeped in through the walls, rising faster than anyone expected. The carpet soaked; the walls warped, and within hours the entire basement was destroyed.

I watched my belongings floating, damp and ruined, and strangely, instead of panic, I felt an overwhelming sense of release. It was as if God Himself had reached down and pulled me out of a place I had stayed for far too long.

The damage forced me to move out immediately. I packed what I could, placed everything inside a storage unit, and for the first time since arriving in America, I stood at a crossroads with no one to tell me what to do next.

This tragedy became my breakthrough. With the help of my dear friend Onye sister, who walked with me from apartment to apartment, I found a humble one bedroom in Maryland. I signed my own lease, held the keys in my hand, and breathed out a kind of freedom I had never tasted before. DGM church youths and young adults came together to help me move in, proof that God always provides the right people at the right time.

Life was not easy. I worked every job I could find, census work, Shoppers Food Warehouse, Wendy's, McDonald's, temp agencies, anything to keep the lights on. Some months, I barely survived. A family friend, Pastor and Mrs. K, paid my rent one month when I couldn't manage it. I paid them back later, but their kindness kept me from losing everything. Mr. and Mrs. Bishop often opened the church food bank freezer to me, making sure I had enough to eat. Those years were humbling, stretching, refining. But they were mine. And they were free.

Ngozi completed high school and went on to college. She became the first beacon of victory in a life that had been riddled with hardship. When she graduated from the university, she came to my Maryland apartment, this time as a young woman, and told me she was ready to hear the truth about her life.

So I sat her down and shared everything: her conception, her birth, the circumstances surrounding Felix, the lies, the secrets, the survival. The truth shook her deeply. She stayed inside the apartment for nearly a week, silent, processing the story of who she truly was.

I had waited because I wanted her to be matured enough. I feared what the truth might do to her. I wanted her to focus on her studies, her future, her dreams, not the pain of her past. Watching her sit quietly for those days broke me and healed me at the same time. She was no longer a child. She was a woman learning her own history.

And we would walk through the next chapter of life together, finally as mother and daughter, in truth, in freedom, and in God's grace.

Leaving that house was not the end of my story; it was the beginning of a new kind of truth. For years, I had carried the weight of silence, believing I was protecting my child by holding my pain alone. But freedom does not come from hiding the past; it comes from meeting it with honesty, love, and care.

When the time was right, I chose to tell my daughter the truth, not to burden her, but to give her clarity, identity, and peace. What followed was not destruction, as I once feared, but understanding. Her response showed me something I had prayed for all her life: that truth, when wrapped in love, has the power to heal more than one generation.

INTERLUDE – A DAUGHTER SPEAKS

Finding Myself in the Truth

What follows is my daughter's reflection, written in her own voice, after learning the truth of her identity and choosing peace over pain.

FINDING OUT THE TRUTH of my identity was a paradigm shift, and it came to me in layers. From a very young age, I sensed that things didn't quite add up. I felt different from my siblings, even though I didn't yet have the vocabulary to put those feelings into words. With the exception of my Grandmother, my parents never treated me differently, this awareness was something I felt instinctively, not something that was shown to me.

When I was fourteen years old, I received concrete proof that the woman I had called "mom" all my life was actually my stepmother. When I began asking questions and was told that my "aunt" was, in fact, my biological mother, the revelation was jarring. In some ways, I felt betrayed. I couldn't understand why this truth had been hidden from me. Even though I had long suspected something, being told, even partially, was an entirely different experience.

With this new information came more questions than answers. Over time, I found gratitude in knowing that I had two mothers, two women who loved me. Still, the questions lingered. The next and most obvious one was: Who was my father? At the time, my biological mother, the author, told me she would explain that part of my story when I was older.

It wasn't until I was twenty-two years old that she finally did.

Intuitively, I had always believed that the man I called "dad" for the first eight years of my life was my father. I couldn't imagine it being any other way. But if he was my biological father, the question then became how that came to be. When my mother told me the truth of what happened, I felt disgusted and angry. I realized then that I, too, would have to walk my own path toward forgiveness.

For a long time, I carried guilt and even shame; not because of who I was, but because of where I came from and what he did to my mother. It has been very difficult to separate the image I had of the father I knew from the person who hurt her so deeply. Even today, I find myself compartmentalizing those emotions.

No one chooses the family they are born into, and God knows best. Over time, I have come to a place of peace and acceptance about who I am. Rather than focusing on my lineage, I choose to put my energy into the family I have created into love, healing, and the life I am building forward.

CHAPTER 16

A Mother's Pain, A Daughter's Promise

JUST AS I WAS rebuilding my own life in America; one paycheck, one prayer, and one step at a time, my heart remained tied to the place I came from. No matter how far I traveled, I could never forget my mother Jessie, the woman who carried me, protected me, and suffered more than anyone ever knew. This chapter begins with her story. The story of a mother whose pain shaped mine, and whose strength helped carry me through my darkest days.

My mother Jessie had lived with pain for as long as I could remember. Even as a young girl in Africa, I watched her rub her swollen knees at night, tying them with her headscarf in an attempt to ease the constant ache. She never complained, never allowed her suffering to slow her down. She was a widow, an orphan, and a mother doing everything she could to keep her children alive. Pain was her companion, but strength was her identity.

As the years passed, the pain in her knees worsened until she could no longer walk without wincing. Eventually, she needed surgery. This was something far beyond her reach financially. My eldest brother, Chidi, stepped in to sponsor the first operation while he was still working as a bank manager in Anambra State. His support kept her going for a little while longer, but God soon called him home, leaving our family with a wound that never truly healed.

After Chidi's death, it became my responsibility to continue caring for our mother Jessie. From America, I paid for her additional knee surgeries, hospital bills, medications, and everything she needed to survive. My brothers, their wives, and my nieces and nephews helped care for her physically, while I carried the financial load however God enabled me.

On one of my trips back home, I ordered a walkable wheelchair for my mother. Because one of her legs had become shorter after the surgeries, she needed custom made shoes as well. Watching her struggle broke my heart, but seeing her determination reminded me where my own resilience came from. Jessie had survived so much poverty, widowhood, loss, and pain yet she still found reasons to smile.

For more than twenty years, Jessie could no longer run her restaurant because of her limited mobility. My second brother Beks and his wife took over the business, keeping her legacy alive. And every month, without fail, I sent money home for her feeding, medications, and care. Whatever I earned, even when I was struggling myself, I sent what I could. I refused to let my mother suffer alone.

Jessie's greatest prayer for me, her only daughter, was that I would marry and have a family of my own. It was a wish she held in her heart until her last breath. I had not told her my stories still being kept secret as demanded by my big aunty Margaret.

On one of my visits home, I sat beside her and finally told her everything. My entire story from the day I was taken to America at fourteen, all the pain I endured in Chief Johnson's family that she was married into, all the secrets I carried, all the heartbreak that shaped my life. As I spoke, my mother wept with a grief that pierced the soul. She cursed the family that had abused me, mourning the years she could never get back, the daughter she could not protect. She said she wished for one day to face Margaret and Felix, but God had taken all of them before such a day could ever come.

Still, in her tears, I felt her love and her pride. I had survived. I had endured. I had kept my promise. The promise to stand on my own two feet and take care of her as long as she lived.

For my two living brothers, I offered the same support. I helped them financially in every way I could, wanting them to stand tall as responsible men who could provide for their families with dignity. I wanted our family to rise; not in wealth, but in stability, honor, and peace.

Looking back now, I realize that supporting my mother and brothers was not just a duty, it was healing. It was my way of restoring what life had taken from us. It was a daughter's love repaying the debt of a mother's sacrifice.

And it was the beginning of a new chapter of rebuilding, not just for my family in Africa, but for myself as well.

CHAPTER 17

God's Surprise: A New Beginning

FOR SO MANY YEARS, marriage was a desire I quietly buried. My heart had grown tired. My trust had been stretched thin. After all the pain I endured, especially at the hands of a man who was an ordained pastor, I stopped praying for a husband. I worked, I studied, I provided for my daughter, and I stayed far away from anything that looked like love. In my mind, marriage was for other women… women whose innocence had not been stolen, whose trust had not been shattered, whose dream for a true love has not been broken even once.

I have come to believe that my story with men began and ended in trauma. But God had written something different.

One Sunday morning, a guest pastor visited our church. He preached with a fire that stirred something buried deep in my spirit. His message was about endurance, healing, and God raising beauty from ashes. I listened quietly, not expecting anything new. My heart wasn't looking for revelation, let alone romance.

But when I returned home that afternoon, something unexpected happened. As I walked past the television, the Holy Spirit whispered to me:

"If Pastor Fred asked you to marry him, would you say yes?"

I froze.

"No," I whispered. "I am not pastor's wife material."

And truthfully, after what Felix did to me in my teenage years, any man with the title "pastor" made my whole body tighten with fear. I had no desire to repeat that nightmare.

So, I dismissed the voice and moved on with my day… or at least I tried. Heaven, however, had no intention of being ignored.

Two weeks later, my Pastor Bishop, aka Daddy G.N., called me to his home. After a few moments of small talk, he cleared his throat and said:

"Daughter, God instructed me to introduce you to Pastor Fred."

He admitted he struggled with that instruction. He knew my history. He knew how carefully my heart had been pieced back together. Even his wife, whom I fundly call

Mommy had concerns. But obedience outweighed hesitation.

The moment he said it, something in me sank and rose at the same time. Because I had already heard the same thing from God Himself.

In our culture, a woman does not approach a man, and besides, marrying a widower with children was not the kind of marriage I had prayed for. I had already raised siblings, supported family, and carried the burdens of others my whole life. I did not want to marry into more responsibility.

God was orchestrating something I did not choose. A blessing wrapped in a package I never imagined.

When Pastor Fred and I began talking, there was no pressure, no rush, no religious performance. He was a widower raising four children. He understood loss. He understood responsibility. And he understood what it meant to cling to God during suffering.

He did not treat me like a project. He did not see me through the lens of my past. He saw the healed woman God had restored.

His family traveled across states to meet with my mother and the rest of my family to ask for my hand in marriage and to perform the necessary traditional engagement and paid my dowry.

Within a year and in June, I walked down the aisle. Not as a victim, but as a bride. My daughter stood beside me as my maid of honor. Our children took their places as bridesmaids and groomsmen. And my mother Jessie wept the kind of tears that washed away decades of sorrow.

My big aunty Margaret was angry because I did not seek her consent and approval as with previous suitors, whom she chased away with her demands for taking responsibility for her and her grandchildren.

> Heaven made a decree that day. "The curse ends here. The blessing begins now." Behold I make all things new
>
> Revelation 21:5

We became a blended family of seven. It was beautiful. It was also challenging. Healing takes time. Merging lives requires patience. Part of me felt the old shadow of bondage rising again. It was not because of Fred. It was the thought of raising someone else's children. This triggered memories of the years I spent raising Felix and Denise's children, working too young, and carrying responsibilities I never asked for.

Yet this time, I was not alone. I had a man who prayed with me, not preyed on me. A man after God's own heart, the very thing I had always prayed for. And God, in His humor, even gave me the children I once dreamed of: two boys and two girls, but now three girls.

The marriage was not my rescue, God was. Marriage was part of the reward.

Some expected me to remain broken. Some thought my story ended in trauma. But God had a chapter waiting that hell never saw coming.

When people see me now, standing beside the man God chose for me, they see restoration holding hands with destiny. They see resilience in a wedding gown. They see the fruit of years of warfare.

And I see one truth clearly: Love did not find me through romance. Love found me through God.

Even though God brought joy into my home, the journey was far from simple. Marriage began a new chapter, but it also opened the door to responsibility, sacrifice, and emotional layers I had long avoided. Becoming a wife after forty, and suddenly becoming a mother of five, forced me to confront old wounds, cultural expectations, and the weight of my family's history. What God rebuilt in my life, He was now preparing to test, stretch, and strengthen through my new role as Mrs. Fred.

And that is where the next chapter begins.

CHAPTER 18

Forgiveness: My Hardest Victory

FORGIVENESS was never a single moment for me. It was not a prayer I prayed once and suddenly woke up free. It was a journey that God walked me through, step by painful step. If I tell you that forgiveness came easily, I would be lying. Every fiber in my body wanted justice. My mind replayed memories that should have destroyed me. My heart was filled with wounds so deep that only God Himself could reach down and heal them.

There were days I asked God why He allowed so much evil to happen to a young, innocent girl who loved Him. There were nights I cried until my eyes had no more tears. I was angry. I felt abandoned. I wanted those who hurt me to feel the pain I felt. I wanted God to punish them hard. Then I remembered something very important:

Forgiveness is not saying what they did was right. Forgiveness is refusing to let what they did destroy me. I learned that unforgiveness is a prison, and the door locks from the inside. If I kept holding the pain and hatred, the enemy would win twice. He would harm me through the abuse and harm me again by holding me captive in bitterness.

For years, I lived in silent torture. I cooked meals every day for the very people who hurt me and stole my life. I stood over pots of food while dark thoughts flashed through my mind: "What if I poison this food? Then the suffering ends for everyone, including me." The enemy whispered death into my ears. He told me I was worthless, invisible, and trapped forever. He tried to turn me into what my abusers were.

But every morning, before my feet touched the floor, I prayed: "Lord, give me the strength for just this one day." And every night, through tears, I whispered: "God, if my life must end, let it be by your hand, not mine."

What saved me was the fear of God and the love for him He planted deep within my spirit. Even in my most broken condition, I still loved God too much to trade places with the enemy. I still cared for my daughter. I refused to become a murderer no matter how much I was hurting.

That decision did not make me free. It simply kept me alive long enough for God to free me Himself.

Forgiveness did not come when the abuse stopped. It did not come the day my abuser had a stroke. It did not come when he died. My heart was still bleeding. Trauma can survive long after the abuser is gone.

Forgiveness began when I finally discovered a truth I had never truly believed:

God loved me. Fully. Fiercely. Personally.

And slowly, that love began to reach the places in me that were full of shame, fear, and anger. As the light of God pushed back the darkness, I started to understand another truth, one I had never seen before:

They were broken too. Lost too. Bound by generational curses that controlled them. Tools of darkness, not victors of it.

I had spent years terrified of becoming what they were, but God showed me that the curse would end with me. My daughter would not inherit their darkness. My lineage would not carry their chains. *What tried to destroy me stopped with me.*

> The Bible says, "For if you forgive men their trespasses, your heavenly Father will also forgive you" Matthew 6:14.

I did not forgive because they deserved it. I forgave because God said I deserved freedom, and because my future, and my daughter's future, depended on it.

Jesus suffered an injustice He never deserved. Yet from the cross He said, "Father, forgive them." If my Savior could forgive those who murdered Him, then with His grace, I could forgive those who tried to murder my spirit.

> "I can do all things through Christ who strengthens me". Philippians 4:13.

Forgiveness did not mean I excused their actions. It meant I refused to carry the curse forward. And eventually, God did something I never expected:

He gave me the ability to pray for them. For their souls. For their future generations. For the chains that held them to be broken, just as mine were.

That kind of forgiveness is not human. It is supernatural. It is the freedom Jesus promised when He said,

> "Whom the Son sets free is free indeed."
>
> John 8:36."

And so forgiveness became my weapon. Forgiveness broke the chains the enemy forged. Forgiveness protected my daughter's future. Forgiveness ended the curse with me.

I forgave so I could breathe again. I forgave so I could love again. I forgave so I could live again.

Today, when I look back, I do not see a victim. I see a survivor transformed into a warrior. I see a woman who refused to die under the weight of evil. I see the fingerprints of God turning every plan of the enemy into a testimony of victory.

Forgiveness is not forgetting. It is not excusing. It is not reconciling with danger.

Forgiveness is cutting the rope that ties you to the past. It is stepping into the future God planned before anyone had a chance to hurt you.

If you, dear reader, are holding pain so deep you can hardly speak about it, I understand. I have been there. Let me tell you this truth:

You do not forgive because they are worth it. You forgive because you are God's child.

I stand today as proof that God can take the most broken heart and rebuild it into something beautiful. Forgiveness was my hardest victory, but also my greatest liberation.

What the enemy meant for evil, God turned for my good. To save lives. Including my own. Genesis 50:20

But forgiveness, though powerful, did not end the battle. It unlocked the door to my freedom, but the enemy did not surrender quietly.

The moment God began to heal my heart; the enemy shifted his attack to my mind.

Forgiveness broke the chains, but my thoughts were still swollen with years of pain, fear, and lies. Even as God began restoring me, the enemy whispered louder, trying desperately to pull me back into the darkness I was fighting so hard to escape.

What came next was a war no one could see. A war for my sanity. A war for my identity. A war for my very life.

And that war, is where my next chapter begins.

CHAPTER 19

The Battle for My Mind

LOOKING BACK now, with healing and distance, I can finally describe the battle that once raged silently inside my mind.

There was a time in my life when the only thing louder than my heartbeat was the voice of despair. I survived each day on the thin thread of hope that God would step in and change my story. My outer world looked ordinary to anyone passing by. I cooked meals, cared for children, cleaned rooms, and smiled when people expected me to. Yet inside, I felt like I was dying piece by piece.

I was trapped in a life that felt like a cage. A place where fear followed me like a shadow. I often asked God if He could see me, if He cared, if He remembered that I was still a child who wanted joy, school, and peace. The weight of being powerless pressed down on me until I could barely breathe.

During those dark years, dangerous thoughts began to creep into my mind. I woke up each morning wishing I had not awakened at all. I believed that everyone's lives, including my own, would be easier if I disappeared. That was the enemy whispering. He wanted me to see death as the only escape.

There were even moments when he tried to twist my pain into anger strong enough to harm others. Since I was the one who prepared meals daily, I battled thoughts telling me to destroy the very people who demanded my obedience. It shocked me that such thoughts could exist inside of me. I had always loved God. I had always wanted to do what was right. Yet pain can push a person to the edge of their strength.

Every time those thoughts came, God pulled me back. I would remember that killing was a sin, and that Hell was real. I would think about my soul and the daughter I carried inside me. I would think about the God I feared and loved. That fear of God saved lives. It saved mine too. The enemy wanted to turn me into someone unrecognizable. God refused to let that happen.

With each passing year, the internal struggle grew heavier. Though I prayed often, answers did not come as fast as my suffering. Sometimes the silence hurt almost as much as the situation. I wondered why God allowed me to stay in a place where cruelty ruled. I wondered if He heard me at all.

He did.

Slowly, I realized that the enemy was not attacking me because I was weak. He was attacking me because he saw the power inside me. He saw the purpose God placed in me. He knew who I would become. He recognized what God had planned long before I did.

There was a voice, quiet but unwavering, that would rise up inside me whenever I came close to giving up. It was the Holy Spirit reminding me:

You are not forgotten. You are not alone. You are not done.

That voice became my lifeline. It kept me breathing. It kept me sane. It kept me alive long enough to recognize the truth that changed everything.

This battle was never about destroying me. It was about preventing my destiny.

The enemy wanted me dead because he feared the woman I would become. He feared the generations that would rise from my womb. He feared the praise I would give to God when He delivered me.

Looking back now, I no longer see myself as a victim trying to survive. I see a warrior who made it out of a battlefield that should have claimed my life. I see a girl God refused to let the enemy swallow. I see a child God shielded until she was strong enough to fight back.

I survived. Not because the pain was small. Not because I was strong. I survived because God held me up when I could not stand.

To any woman or man reading this who may be struggling to stay alive, **Hold on.**

If you are still breathing, God is still working. If you are still here, your story is not over. You may not see the finish line but God sees the victory that is already prepared for you. Darkness does not win. It never has and it never will.

The fact that you are reading these words is a sign that God is protecting you even now. I should not be here today, yet here I am. Alive. Free. Loved. Chosen. A witness to the power of God.

The enemy tried to take everything from me. He failed.

Because God never let go of my hand.

Today, as I write these words, I no longer live in the shadows of what was done to me. I walk in the light of who God has called me to be. I am healed. I am whole. And, I am free.

Everything the enemy tried to use to bury me became the very ground God used to grow me. My mind is no longer a battlefield; it is a place of peace, clarity, and strength. My heart is no longer a home for fear; it is a home for God's love. My life is no longer shaped by trauma, it is shaped by purpose.

If God could rescue a broken girl trapped in silence and turn her into a woman of power, He can rescue you too. Your story is not over. Your healing is not impossible. Your future is not destroyed and cannot be. The same God who held me together is the same God who will carry you through every storm.

This is not just my testimony. It is my victory cry. And it is your promise.

The enemy fought hard. But God fought harder. And God won.

CHAPTER 20

The Year I Finally Chose Myself

ALL OF MY LIFE, it has always been about sacrificing myself for others and taking care of other people but, nothing for myself with all the many years spent in America. So, for my fiftieth birthday, the now Mrs. Fred, I wanted to do something for myself instead of just having an elaborate expensive birthday party that has no lasting reward. I shared my heart's wish with my older cousin Uche in California who promised to help me achieve my goal.

At first, it seemed like my wish wasn't going to be realized so, I decided to go on a one-week vacation all by myself. While on vacation, my older cousin Uche called informing me that my wish may be possible. Then suddenly with the help of God and cousin Uche, I was able to complete a small project in my hometown; a house of my own, where I can freely go to anytime and relax without feeling obligated to any human being whatsoever except to God and God alone – hallelujah! My own country home!!

When the project was completed and I was slated to visit the homeland, the devil did try to steal, kill and destroy my life with death disguised in the form of seizures. The year that I planned to visit the newly completed home project in Africa. It was then that I recognized the parallel ancestral curse. The same incident happened with my late eldest brother, Chidi. When Chidi had completed his home project, instead of moving into the new home alive, Chidi transitioned and he entered his new home in a casket. So, when I saw the same ancestral handwriting on the wall, everything was tackled in the spirit through fasting, prayers by intercessory men and women of God whom I trusted and could confide in. John 10:10 The thief cometh not, but for to steal, and to kill, and to destroy. I am come that they might have life, and that they might have it more abundantly.

Ngozi also completed her very own Master's degree as well to God's glory. Furthermore, to God's glory, my only daughter Ngozi did also get married to a blessed God fearing man of her own choice by God's grace. Ngozi and her beloved husband William are blessed by God with a precious, miraculous son Chinwenmeri thereby making us a very happy and blessed grandparents to God's honor and glory! Ngozi has always wanted to visit Africa ever since she was a little girl. But, because I had no place of my own, I could not take Ngozi to Africa to see or visit her biological Grandmother Jessie though they used to talk over the phone when her grandma Jessie was alive with me interpreting for both of them.

As God would have it, not only did I step my foot alive into the new home but, Ngozi (the second generation), with her husband William and their son Chinwemeri (the third generation) were all able to witness and step all our feet alive into the blessed, miraculous home from God. Thank you Lord that I became the final and last destination for all the ancestral curses to proceed no further in my lineage and future generations to come, Amen! The rest of our four children are now grown adults, still trying to figure out life for themselves as we are all a work in progress each day until the Lord God calls each one home to eternity forever.

I couldn't help but notice how the Almighty Father God took me as a teenager from my mother Jessie in the village of Africa and brought me to the land of opportunity, the USA. It was the same way He took Joseph and Queen Esther in the Bible to another country. He used us as instruments to save our immediate families and God's people. God has brought me and my offspring through so many life-threatening health challenges that if God had not brought us to America, we might not have been in existence to tell this testimony to encourage God's children and to God's glory alone!

CHAPTER 21

Breaking Curses and Claiming Destiny

STEPPING INTO MARRIAGE after forty felt like stepping into a promise I never expected God to fulfill. After all the pain, betrayal, and disappointment, I thought that kind of blessing wasn't meant for someone like me. But as beautiful as that new chapter was, it did not erase the battles I had been fighting long before love found me. Becoming a wife brought joy, but it also uncovered layers of responsibility, old wounds, and spiritual assignments I did not yet understand.

It took me years to realize that the struggles I fought in silence were not just my own. The patterns of pain in my life had roots that stretched beyond my childhood, beyond my mother, beyond even my grandmother. I had inherited battles that began long before I was born, cycles of abuse, loss, betrayal, and unfinished destinies. In my family, joy was often followed by tragedy. Breakthroughs were often met with sudden death. Blessings seemed to disappear right at the finish line. I saw this most painfully through my older brother. He worked tirelessly to build a home he was proud of, a home that was meant to symbolize a new beginning for our family. But before he ever slept one night inside, death took him. His casket was placed in the house he built with his own hands. I did not understand it then, but now I see the truth with clarity. The enemy killed him at the finish line.

Years later, that same pattern tried to repeat itself through me.

After surviving an unspeakable torment in America, after finding my footing, raising my daughter, and pursuing my education, I was finally preparing to visit Africa. I wanted my daughter to know her roots. I wanted to show my family that I had survived what was meant to destroy me. I wanted them to see God's mercy with their own eyes, new home.

But as soon as the trip was set, the enemy showed his hand.

One day, without warning, I collapsed. My body stiffened. I suffered a seizure. Fear surrounded me like a thick blanket. In that moment, the enemy intended for my story to end like my brother's. He wanted my body shipped back to Africa, not my living testimony. He wanted to bury me before I could walk into the land God wanted to restore. Before I could step my foot in my new home.

But here is what the enemy did not understand:

I had already died in my spirit years ago. And God had resurrected me. He could not kill what God had brought back to life.

When I recovered, I knew this was not just a medical event. It was spiritual warfare. It was a final attempt to stop me from returning home and reclaiming the territory the enemy had stolen from my family for generations. I had a few more episodes, but nothing was found medically wrong with me.

I stood in our home, trembling but unshaken, and declared:

"If I am going to Africa, I will go on my feet and alive.

I will not return as a dead body. The curse ends with me."

And God honored my declaration. Job 22:28 declares:

> Thou shalt decree a thing, and it shall be established unto thee, and the light shall shine upon thy way.

Not only did I travel to Africa, but I also traveled with my daughter. Three living generations walking into a place death thought would receive us in a coffin. That journey was not a trip; it was a victory march. A divine reversal of old curses. Generational curses are broken.

I walked the roads my ancestors walked. I stood in the home my brother never lived in and spent the days in mine. I touched the soil where generational pain was planted. I declared, out loud and with boldness:

"My bloodline will live and not die."

I laid hands on my daughter and prayed. I stood before my mother's grave and spoke life. I walked through the places where death thought it had triumphed.

And God revealed something I never understood before:

I was not cursed. I was chosen. I was the warrior God selected to stop what destroyed those before me.

When I returned to America, the attacks did not stop immediately. Curses do not break quietly, they break violently, shaking everything before they release their grip. But little by little, year by year, I began to see fruit that once seemed impossible:

A daughter protected. A mother honored. A marriage blessed. A career established. A home filled with peace instead of trauma. Life multiplying in the very places death once reigned.

Today, when I look at my children, both the ones I birthed, and the ones God gave me through marriage, I see generations rising from the ground the enemy hoped would be our graves.

I now understand why the enemy fought me so fiercely: He saw the legacy I would build. He saw the destinies I would influence. He saw the spiritual inheritance waiting behind my obedience. He saw the houses that would be lived in, not buried in. He saw the ministries, the breakthroughs, the generational blessings.

The curse that killed my brother could not kill me. The curse that tormented my family could not bind my future. The curse that tried to swallow our lineage has been stripped of its power.

I did not break it by might. God broke it by His promise. And He used my survival as the weapon.

> "The Lord is my strength and My song and is become my salvation" Psalm 118:14.

To every woman or man who fears that their children will repeat their pain, hear me clearly:

You are not the curse. You are the warrior God chose to destroy it.

The enemy tried to bury us. But God turned us into seeds in the ground. And from those seeds, generations will rise.

"Except a corn of wheat fall into the ground and die, it abideth alone, but if it dies, it bringeth forth much fruit." Matthew 12:24

The curse ends here. And legacy begins now.

CHAPTER 22

God Is Always on Time

MY INTENTION for writing this book is to admonish my fellow Christian brothers and sisters in the Lord Jesus Christ that with God, all things are possible, Matthew 19:26 "But Jesus beheld them, and said unto them, with men this is impossible; but with God all things are possible". And, when God is for you, who can be against you, Romans 8:31 "What shall we then say to these things? If God be for us, who can be against us?".

Be encouraged beloved brethren in Christ Jesus! No matter what trials, tribulations, tests, circumstances, or situations you are going through today or may yet go through in this earthly life, our Almighty Father God is aware of them all. God through his beloved and only son, Jesus Christ, shall certainly bring you, and us through it all. God is the Alpha and the Omega in all of our lives and no one else, Hallelujah! Revelation 1:8 "I am Alpha and

Omega, the beginning and the ending, saith the Lord, which is, and which was, and which is to come, the Almighty."

This book is dedicated to my mother, the late orphan Jessie, to state that all of your sufferings and sacrifices since childhood in this earthly life were not in vain. Your legacy lives on for many more generations to come and, may your gentle soul continue to rest peacefully in the bosom of our Lord and Savior Jesus Christ, Amen!

EPILOGUE

My Heart's Reflection

THERE WERE MANY MOMENTS in my life when I thought my story would end in silence, in pain, or in the shadows of things I never asked for. But God had a different ending in mind. The battles I walked through were not meant to destroy me, they were meant to shape me into a vessel He could use.

I wrote these chapters as a testimony, but also as an invitation. An invitation to anyone who feels unseen. To anyone carrying silent wounds. To anyone who has cried prayers that seemed unanswered. To anyone who has questioned their purpose or their worth. To anyone who has survived what should have killed them.

If my life has taught me anything, it is this:

God never abandons His children. He never wastes pain. He never lets trauma have the final word.

Every scar I carry has become a medal of victory. Every tear I cried became a seed for my healing. Every attack of the enemy became evidence of the destiny God placed within me.

I am not who I was. I am not what was done to me. I am not the sum of my darkest days.

I am who God says I am. Chosen. Loved. Protected. Redeemed. Restored. And destined for greatness.

If you have walked through this book with me, chapter by chapter, memory by memory, miracle by miracle, thank you. Thank you for allowing me to open the most vulnerable parts of my soul. Thank you for listening, for feeling, for witnessing what God has done in me.

My hope is that my testimony will stir something inside you; a spark of courage, a whisper of hope, a reminder that you are not alone.

This is not the end of my story. And if you are reading this, it is not the end of yours.

You were created for more. You were chosen for a purpose. You were destined to rise.

And just as God carried me through every fire, He will carry you too.

This book closes here, but your new beginning starts now.

CLOSING PRAYER

For the Reader

HEAVENLY FATHER,

I lift up the one who is reading this prayer right now. You know their story. You know their battles. You know their heartbreaks, their hidden wounds, and their silent prayers.

Lord, surround them with Your love in this very moment. Wrap Your presence around them like a blanket. Let them feel the warmth of Your peace, the strength of Your protection, and the power of Your healing.

Break every chain that has tried to hold them captive. Silence every lie spoken against them. Destroy every generational curse that has followed their family line. And release Your freedom, Your clarity, and Your restoration into their life.

Father, renew their mind. Calm every storm in their heart. Fill every empty place with your spirit. Where there has been fear, give faith. Where there has been shame, give dignity. Where there has been trauma, give deliverance. Where there has been loss, give overflow.

Remind them that they are your child. Chosen. Loved. Seen. And never forgotten.

I speak life over them. I speak victory over them. I speak healing over them. I speak peace over them.

May they rise from this moment stronger than they've ever been. May they walk into their destiny with confidence. May they know that the enemy's attacks were proof of the power inside them. And may they live the rest of their days protected, guided, and anchored in your love.

Lord, thank you for what you have done in their life. Thank you for what you are doing right now. And thank you for the miracles that are on their way.

In Jesus' mighty name, Amen.

ABOUT THE AUTHOR

ESTHER CHARITY OSEMWEGIE is a woman shaped by fire, strengthened by faith, and carried by the hand of God. A survivor of childhood trauma, spiritual warfare, and generational bondage. She has become a living testimony of God's power to redeem, restore, and rewrite a life the enemy tried to destroy.

Born in Africa and raised between two worlds, Esther's journey has taken her from hidden suffering to bold, unapologetic victory. Today, she is a wife, mother, grandmother, intercessor, and warrior for Christ. Her life's calling is to break chains, expose darkness, and help others discover the healing, hope, and destiny found only in God.

Esther writes with transparency, courage, and compassion, offering her testimony as a lighthouse for anyone walking through deep waters. She believes in the power of prayer, the reality of spiritual warfare, and the unstoppable grace of God that carried her from survival to purpose.

Her story is not just her own. It is proof that God sees, God saves, and God restores.

Continue the Journey

The African Girl God Remembered

www.ingramcontent.com/pod-product-compliance
Lightning Source LLC
Chambersburg PA
CBHW070920180426
43192CB00038B/2100